I will give thanks to you, LORD, with all my heart; I will tell of all your wonderful deeds.

- Psalm 9:1 (NIV)

Tales
FROM THE
Leaf Pile

A Holiday Road Devotional

By Jason Byerly

FLANIGAN
PRESS

Scripture quotations marked (NIV) are taken from the Holy Bible, New International Version®, NIV®. Copyright © 1973, 1978, 1984, 2011 by Biblica, Inc.™ Used by permission of Zondervan. All rights reserved worldwide. www.zondervan.com The "NIV" and "New International Version" are trademarks registered in the United States Patent and Trademark Office by Biblica, Inc.™

Scripture quotations are taken from the Holy Bible, New Living Translation, copyright ©1996, 2004, 2007, 2013, 2015 by Tyndale House Foundation. Used by permission of Tyndale House Publishers, Inc., Carol Stream, Illinois 60188. All rights reserved.

Scripture quotations from THE MESSAGE. Copyright © by Eugene H. Peterson 1993, 1994, 1995, 1996, 2000, 2001, 2002. Used by permission of NavPress. All rights reserved. Represented by Tyndale House Publishers, Inc.

Cover art adapted from a vector by Svetosila/shutterstock.
Artwork on journal page and chapter pages by mire/shutterstock and KsanaGaphica/shutterstock.
Artwork on bonus section page by vecteezy.com.

First Printing, 2017
The author owns all rights to the devotions in this book but wishes to acknowledge that some of the work is adapted from the author's columns that previously appeared in *Southern Indiana Living Magazine*, *The Clarion News* and in the ebook *The Life Less Traveled*, 2011.

Flanigan Press

ISBN: 978-0692960905 (paperback)

www.jasonbyerly.com

For Christy.

Grateful for the memories of so
many cozy autumns together.

CONTENTS

INTRODUCTION

I took my family to a festival at a local park on Sunday, and it felt like a thousand degrees in the shade. The place was packed with people, which just made it hotter. It was such a scorcher that I had to carry my dog across the parking lot to keep her from burning her paws.

On days like that, autumn seems like a distant mirage. Who could imagine throwing on a sweater or making s'mores by a bonfire when the temperature is pushing 90?

Yet, there I was standing in line for ice cream when I saw it. A single leaf seesawing its way down from the tree above. It's coming, I thought. Believe it or not, autumn really is on its way.

With the beginning of fall come all of the amazing experiences of the season: raking leaves, carving pumpkins, sipping hot drinks on cool, rainy mornings, and so much more.

My favorite part about autumn, though, is that it's a season of spectacular change. The trees ignite with color. The evening temperatures plummet. And the world looks like a brand new place. It's as if creation is showing us that anything really is possible with God.

Autumn reminds me that I am made by a God who specializes in transformation. Though he never changes, he has more than enough power to help me make the changes I crave.

The Artist who paints the fall leaves is longing to paint a fresh scene in your life and mine. God once told his people, "Forget the former things; do not dwell on the past. See, I am doing a new thing" (Isaiah 43:18-19 NIV). The good news is that he is still in the business of doing new things today.

Whatever seems impossible in your life right now, wherever you may feel stuck, remember that a new season is coming soon, and every day is a brand new day with God. I'm praying that the stories in this book will encourage you to walk with him and enjoy all that he has for you this season.

1

APPLE OF YOUR EYE

Keep me as the apple of your eye;
hide me in the shadow of your wings.

– PSALM 17:8 (NIV)

Every year when the air grows crisp and the leaves turn to fire, my family heads to the local orchard to pick apples. It's one of my favorite family traditions. The road to the orchard winds through horse farms and cow pastures, and we have a contest to see who can count the most animals along the way.

When we get to the orchard, we grab a wagon. It's a good hike to the back of the property to the apple trees, and I always give my daughters a ride. It used to be no big deal, but now my back tells me otherwise. My kids are getting heavy.

Unfortunately, they're also growing tall. In the old days, when my girls were still preschoolers, they couldn't reach the apples on their own. I'd hoist one of them up on my shoulders, and we'd wade into the branches together to find the best fruit. It was the together part that made it fun. They're big enough now to reach the lower branches on their own. We're still picking apples together, but just not as together as we used to be.

As a dad, I love "together." I want to be as close to my kids as possible. Orchards are fine and all, but it's really just an excuse to spend time as a family. The drive, the wagon ride, the apple picking and, later that night, eating apple dumplings after dinner - they're all just props to bring us closer together.

The desire for together comes from God. God loves together. This is nothing new.

In Psalm 17:8, when a king named David found himself in serious trouble, he prayed, "Keep me as the apple of your eye; hide me in the shadow of your wings" (NIV).

Literally, David was asking God to protect him as someone would protect his own eye from danger. Translators, though, use the phrase "apple of my eye" because it refers to something precious to you. It is an object reflected in the pupil of your eye.[1] Why is it reflected? Because you're close to it, and you're looking right at it. In other words, David prayed for God to draw him near and to keep his eye on him.

That's a prayer God is more than happy to answer. He is a God who would rather hoist us on his shoulders than watch us from a distance. He would rather pull us in a wagon behind him than let us walk through life alone. He is a loving dad, and like all loving dads, God loves together.

If you could look into the eyes of God, you'd be sure to see your reflection. His face is turned to you, and he yearns to draw you near. Even if you feel rotten to the core, you are still the apple of God's eye.

And you know what they say about apples, right? They never fall far from the tree. No matter how far we fall, no matter much we think we've blown it, we're never as far from God as we think. An apple a day may keep the doctor away, but nothing can separate us from a Father who loves us and longs to do life together.

So this fall, whether you make it to an orchard or prefer to pick your produce in the store, grab an apple, and let it remind you that you are precious in the eyes of God.

Journal Prompts

Who are the people in your life you love to spend time with the most? What are your favorite things to do together?

How does it make you feel to know that God wants to be close to you? When have you felt closest to him?

Is there anything in your life right now that's making you feel distant from God? Who can you talk to about it?

God, thank you for loving me. I want to be as close to you as possible. Draw me near, and help me to watch out for anything that would distract me from you.

Amen

2

S'MORE GOD

Open your mouth wide and I will fill it with good things.

- PSALM 81:10 (NLT)

My friend Mandy had never eaten a s'more until she had one at a bonfire last fall. I was excited for her to say the least. It was like meeting someone raised on a desert island who had never heard of electricity but got to see a light bulb turned on for the very first time. I bet Mandy looked a lot like that when she ate her first s'more.

I have other friends who will make s'mores out of anything. Reese's Peanut Butter Cups, Caramello bars, Rolos, even Nutella. I, however, am a purist. Give me a golden brown marshmallow, a couple of graham crackers and a Hershey bar. This is the way God clearly intended it, and who am I to mess with God's creation? I pray for my Reese's friends daily.

Nobody really knows where s'mores originated, though they were definitely big with the Girl Scouts by the early twentieth century.[2] The name, of course, comes from the fact when you eat this campfire treat, they taste so good you want some more. I think if you only eat one, you can't properly call it a s'more. It's just a s'one, and who wants to eat a s'one?

Even though the invention of the s'more is a mystery, the principle of the s'more has been around for a long time. When you stumble on a good thing, you can't help but want some more. You see that idea all throughout the Bible.

The psalmists urge us to "Taste and see that the Lord is good" (Psalm 34:8 NLT) and compare God's Word with dessert. "How sweet are your words to my taste, sweeter than honey to my mouth" (Psalm 119:103 NIV).

They also paint a picture of physical longing for the presence of God, "O God, you are my God; I earnestly search for you. My soul thirsts for you; my whole body longs for you in this parched and weary land where there is no water" (Psalm 63:1 NLT).

God is more than happy to satisfy this longing for his presence. "Open your mouth wide," he promised his people, "and I will fill it with good things" (Psalm 81:10 NLT).

When I first met God in college, I was like my friend Mandy and her s'more. I'd heard about God all my life, but once I tried him for myself, I was hooked. I couldn't settle for a s'one God. My experience of God's love and presence was so delicious I had to have s'more. Still do. A little taste of God's just not enough, and I when I get busy and try to skimp on my time with him, I get irritable.

Some folks are like this when you take their chocolate away. They may lose weight on a diet, but they're no fun to be around. I'm like that with God. Don't just give me a nibble of him. I've tasted and seen that the Lord is good, and I will not be satisfied unless I get s'more.

Journal Prompts

What is your favorite dessert? When do you crave it the most?

What are some things you love about God? Spend a few minutes telling him what you love about him right now.

How can you get more of God in your life? Are there any regular practices like praying, reading your Bible or listening to worship music that would help satisfy that craving?

God, I want more of you in my life.
Come and fill my heart with good things.
Help me to remember that no one
and nothing can satisfy my soul like you.

Amen

3

Secrets of the Squirrel Whisperer

His sheep follow him because they know his voice.

– John 10:4 (NIV)

You know fall is right around the corner when the squirrels shift into high gear. Even as I write this they are swarming my neighborhood gathering food for winter. I once met a squirrel, though, who didn't have to work as hard as the ones who live on my street. That's because he had a special friend.

I call her the Squirrel Whisperer. Her family calls her Auntie. She is my wife's great-aunt, and I have watched her tame rodents with her beguiling charm. Impossible, you say? I once thought so myself, until I saw it with my own eyes.

The only time we see Auntie is when we visit the family cabins nestled in the foothills of the Smoky Mountains where the squirrels run thicker than mud.

"Auntie has a pet squirrel," my wife told me during one visit. She said this casually as if she were referring to a cat.

"What are you talking about?" I asked. Surely, I'd misunderstood. "Did you say a squirrel?"

"Yeah, it eats right from her hand," she said. This I had to see.

Auntie, silver-haired and spry, stood on the deck of her cabin, peanuts in hand and called him, "Chht-chht-chht! Chht-chht-chht! Here, Squirrely! Here, Squirrely, Squirrely!"

I was convinced she'd lost her mind.

But then Squirrely popped his head out from the branch of tree. Maybe I was the one losing my mind. I watched in disbelief as Squirrely climbed to the ground, pranced right up to her, and snatched a peanut from her hand. He wiggled his tail at her and skittered off.

I had never seen anything quite like it. Even when Auntie was gone for the day, Squirrely would hang out by her cabin waiting to greet her when she came home like a loyal golden retriever.

I tried to call Squirrely once myself, just to see how hard it was to get on his good side, but he would have nothing to do with me. We just didn't have the same relationship.

One day Auntie called Squirrely to introduce him to my daughters. The squirrel came halfway down the tree, got spooked and bolted.

"What's wrong?" I asked.

She looked at me matter-of-factly and answered, "That's not Squirrely."

Squirrely knew her voice and she, apparently, knew his.

In the Bible, Jesus made a similar claim about his sheep. "I am the Good Shepherd. I know my sheep and my sheep know me" (John 10:14 NIV).

I don't know much about sheep, but some days the squirrel seems like a better metaphor for my spiritual life. I'm relationally skittish and find it hard to get close to people. I don't trust easily. And, like a squirrel, I have a tendency to hoard my stuff.

Yet, there is a voice that calls to me and, when I take time to listen, reassures me I have a friend, a friend who though very different from me, is someone I can trust. Someone who provides for me. Someone who, as mismatched as we may seem, wants to have a relationship with me.

If you think a retired lady and a squirrel make an odd couple, just imagine an infinite, selfless God hanging out with flawed, self-centered humans.

A Good Shepherd. A Squirrel Whisperer. Whatever you want

to call him, he's calling your name today. As hard as it is to believe, there is a God, who though totally beyond you is, in fact, nuts about you.

Journal Prompts

How does it make you feel to realize that God is crazy about you? Is it hard for you to believe? Why or why not?

How does God speak to you? Through the Bible? Prayer? Songs? Wise friends? Do you recognize his voice when you hear it?

Do you take your needs to God or just try to handle life on your own? What do you need to take to him today?

God, you are a Good Shepherd.
Thanks for loving me so much.
Help me to learn to listen to
your voice each and every day.

Amen

4

RAKING LEAVES

So let's not get tired of doing what is good.
At just the right time we will reap a
harvest of blessing if we don't give up.

– GALATIANS 6:9 (NLT)

If you've ever wondered where leaves go when they're blowing down the street, I can tell you. They end up by my front door. My house and my next-door neighbor's are built at the exact perfect angle to funnel every stray leaf in my zip code directly to my doorstep. It's a precisely engineered wind tunnel.

This is a great selling point for my house for people who like to jump into leaf piles. It's a pain for anyone who has to rake them. It doesn't matter how many times you tackle the leaves by my door, they magically return within a couple of days.

Sometimes it even happens while I'm raking. One day I was out scooping up leaves into our yard waste bin when the wind kicked up and dumped a fresh pile of leaves right at my feet. I thought about just lighting them on fire.

It makes me think about how the wise man Solomon once summed up all human activity on earth. He said, "I observed everything going on under the sun, and really, it is all meaningless—like chasing the wind" (Ecclesiastes 1:14 NLT).

This guy must have been a lot of fun at parties. But, hey, I get what he's saying. Some days it seems like no matter how hard we work, we don't make much of a difference in the world around us.

Whether it's our yard work, our jobs, or even our closest relationships, it sometimes feels like we're giving life our best but not seeing much progress. It's all effort and no payoff. We bust our tails at work but get passed over for promotions and raises. We pour time into our marriage, our kids, and our friendships only to face conflict and unmet expectations.

Even our relationship with God can be frustrating. How long, we wonder, are we going to struggle with the same old temptations? We read our Bible, pray, and do our best to follow God, yet sometimes it seems like we're not growing much at all.

We rake, we rake, we rake and at the end of the day, we understand what Solomon was saying, because it all feels like we're chasing after the wind.

During times like this I have to remind myself that God's perspective is different than mine. We may not think we're making progress in life. We may not think we're making much of a difference, but we're so limited by the narrow scope of our vision. God sees the big picture, the whole earth, the universe, and all of time laid out before him. All we see is our yard.

"'For my thoughts are not your thoughts, neither are your ways my ways,' declares the Lord. 'As the heavens are higher than the earth, so are my ways higher than your ways, and my thoughts than your thoughts'" (Isaiah 55:8-9 NIV).

We may be frustrated at work but fail to see the lives we're touching or even the difference we're making just by showing up and doing our job to the best of our ability. Your boss may not notice, but God sure does.

Our relationships might be less than perfect, but that doesn't mean we're not making a positive impact on our spouses, kids, and friends for the long haul. We often don't know how much we've touched someone's life until years down the road.

And when it comes to our spiritual growth, this is the easiest one to miss of all. We grow in fits and starts, taking three steps forward and two steps back. Like a plant in early spring, all the growth is happening beneath the surface, and even though the ground may look barren, miraculous things are happening down in the soil of our hearts.

The apostle Paul had something like this in mind when he gave us this advice, "So let's not get tired of doing what is good. At just the right time we will reap a harvest of blessing if we don't give up" (Galatians 6:9 NLT).

So I guess I'll keep on raking, keep on working, and keep on loving even if the leaves blow back into my yard tomorrow. My job is just to show up and be faithful, and I'll trust God to work out the rest.

Journal Prompts

Is there any place in your life you feel like you're not making a difference? What makes you feel this way?

How do you think God sees the situation? Where might you be making a bigger difference than you realize?

Do you know anyone else who feels like they're "chasing the wind" right now? How could you encourage them to not give up?

God, thanks for your encouragement today.
Please remind me that my life counts and help me to stay
faithful even on those days when I feel like giving up.

Amen

5

THE (NOT SO) PERFECT PUMPKIN PIE

People judge by outward appearance, but the Lord looks at the heart.

- 1 SAMUEL 16:7 (NLT)

Not just anyone can fix a good pumpkin pie. Oh I know the recipe is simple enough, but you have to be paying attention or you can ruin it. That's what happened on my daughter's birthday a few years ago.

When you have a fall birthday in my house, you don't always get a normal cake. Sometimes you get pie, which is not an altogether bad deal, unless, like I said, someone messes it up.

My wife meant well, but she had a lot going on. We were packing to leave town for a few days, and she was just trying to do too many things at once. When she pulled the pie out of the oven, the edge of the crust was almost burned.

She thought it was fine, but I couldn't let it go. This was my daughter's birthday cake for crying out loud. I wanted it to be picture perfect. "Don't worry about it," I said. "I've got this."

So, I grabbed a new pie crust, whipped the ingredients together and popped it in the oven. I, however, wasn't going to make the same mistake my wife did. I stood by the oven and watched it like a hawk.

When the timer went off, I pulled it out, and I don't mean to brag here, but this pie looked so good it would have made Martha Stewart weep with envy. The crust was golden brown, and the custard was baked to a deep caramel color, its nearly flawless surface ever-so-slightly cracked around the edges, cooked to perfection.

The pie was so beautiful that I didn't know whether to put it on the table or donate it to a museum. However, since it was my daughter's birthday, I figured she should actually get to try a bite. I just hoped my wife didn't feel too bad about me showing her up in the kitchen.

After lunch, we put candles in the pie and sang "Happy Birthday," and it was finally time to enjoy the fruit of my labor. I couldn't wait to dig in. I served up a slice to the whole family and, being the servant that I am, went to the fridge to grab some whipped cream before I tasted it myself.

Just as I opened the refrigerator door, my wife yelled, "Don't eat that!" Wow, I knew she'd be jealous, but this was a bit much. When I saw the look on everyone's face, however, I knew something was wrong.

That's when it hit me. I'd left out the sugar.

I couldn't believe it. I tried it myself just to see how bad it really was, and I nearly gagged. In case you've ever wondered, sugarless pumpkin pie is disgusting.

Fortunately we had a back up. My wife pulled out her rejected pie, and even though it wasn't picture perfect, it was absolutely delicious.

No surprise there. After all, there was a law of the universe at work that day that applies to both pies and people. It's what's on the inside that counts, or as God said it in 1 Samuel 16:7, "People judge by outward appearance, but the Lord looks at the heart" (NLT).

You can be beautiful on the outside, but if your heart's not right, it won't long take for people to figure it out. And, of course, the opposite is true. Even on those days when you're feeling a little burnt around the edges, a heart sweetened by the love of God is a delicious treat for anyone who comes near your table.

Journal Prompts

Do you spend more time focusing on your outward appearance or on the condition of your heart?

How's your heart right now? Is it sweetened by God's love or are there any areas of bitterness you need to surrender to him?

Do you ever struggle with your appearance or self-image? Take a look at Psalm 139:14 and Ephesians 2:10. Describe yourself as God sees you.

God, you know the real me.
Please show me what's in my heart
and anything you want to change.
Transform me from the inside out today.

Amen

6

SCHOOL SUPPLIES

By his divine power, God has given us everything
we need for living a godly life.

- 2 PETER 1:3 (NLT)

I didn't always love school, but I loved buying school supplies. They were my consolation prize for having to give up my summer vacation. One of the greatest rituals of fall was going to the store with my mom and loading up on crayons, markers, and big, fat erasers that could fix any mistake.

Of all this equipment, however, none could compete with the Trapper Keeper. It was like the Swiss Army Knife of back-to-school gear. Not only was it a three-ring binder that held your loose-leaf notebook paper in place, not only did it have a million folders and pockets that kept random notes from falling out, and not only did it have a clipboard in the back and conversion tables printed inside the folders that looked like you were preparing for a NASA launch, but it even had one of those cool plastic pouches that held protractors, scissors and pencil sharpeners.

It was a thing of beauty. With my Trapper Keeper I was prepared for any situation that might come my way. If only they made such a device to help us deal with the everyday challenges of the grown-up world. Maybe we could call it the Sanity Keeper because it would help us to stay sane when life gets crazy.

Fighting with your spouse? Get out your Sanity Keeper and find the conversion chart that tells you the right thing to say. Discouraged at your job? Look in the pocket of your Sanity Keeper for the encouragement to help you bounce back. Struggling with anxiety? Check the clipboard of your Sanity Keeper for a healthy dose of reality that puts those anxieties in perspective.

The good news is there really is such a Sanity Keeper. It's called the Bible, and it is the spiritual Swiss Army Knife that helps us to survive and thrive in our daily lives. Jesus' friend Peter assures us that "By his divine power, God has given us everything we need for living a godly life" (2 Peter 1:3 NLT). Peter goes on to say that God's promises are the keys to experiencing that life, a life that doesn't settle for the same old junk the world throws at us, but enables us to live a better story.

I don't know about you, but I don't always live like that's true. I forget that my Sanity Keeper is fully loaded with everything I need to live out the life God offers me. I haven't been given a shabby manila folder to get me through my day, but a strategically designed binder with 66 pockets packed with wisdom to help me handle anything life throws my way.

True confession time: I still have the last Trapper Keeper my parents bought me tucked away in my closet. I just can't give it up. It reminds me of those back-to-school shopping trips and autumn days when all that I needed in life could be stashed away in a three-ring binder. I don't get it out much anymore, though. These days I turn to my Sanity Keeper to help me remember God's promises, rely on his wisdom, and walk with him each day through the school of life.

Journal Prompts

What's the craziest thing going on in your life right now? Where do you need the most help?

What does the Bible have to say about this situation? Is there one of God's promises that could encourage you?

If you're not familiar with the Bible or just want to go deeper, who can help you to learn more?

God, thank you for the Bible
and for the way you use it to keep me sane
even on the craziest of days. Please help me
to make it the first place I always go
to deal with the challenges of life.

Amen

7

HAY RIDE

Peace I leave with you; my peace I give you.
I do not give to you as the world gives.
Do not let your hearts be troubled and do not be afraid.

– JOHN 14:27 (NIV)

I love hayrides but I refuse to go on any of the ones where people try to scare you. It would be a total waste of money for me because I have kids who jump out and scare me all of the time. They think it's hilarious.

They hide behind doors, under tables and in any other space they can wedge themselves into where they wait for me to pass by. Then they spring on me and scream in my face. I thought it was just a phase they were going through, but now it's a way of life.

I go on hayrides to get away from all of that. It's the one place where I can keep an eye on my children at all times. No scares allowed.

That's why I don't go for the haunted hayride experience. For me, hayrides should be a relaxing trip through the countryside, not somewhere I have to be on guard against ghosts and goblins. I want to hear the steady drone of a tractor or the clip-clop of horseshoes on packed earth, not a teen-age girl screaming in my ear.

That's not to say, however, that all of my hayrides have been dull.

When I was a kid, my uncle loaded the bed of his pickup with straw, invited a bunch of us to climb in the back and took us flying around the county on narrow, gravel roads. I don't think we had much straw by the end, but at least most of us were still in the truck.

My wife loves to remind me of the story of the first hayride we ever took together. According to her, I spent the entire ride talking to another girl. I honestly don't remember that, and, in my defense, I thought Christy was already taken. But that sounds like something dumb I might do: sit three feet away from the girl of my dreams and almost totally miss the boat. That was a dangerous hayride in its own right.

Since that day, I've been on plenty of hayrides with my kids, sometimes even supervising children on class trips, which can be an experience so harrowing that it makes even the scariest haunted hayrides look tame by comparison.

I guess that's the way it goes with any ride in life. Even the ones you expect to be peaceful may turn out to be full of twists and turns that you didn't see coming. It reminds me of how a shepherd named David once described his experience with God. David said, "He makes me lie down in green pastures, he leads me beside quiet waters" (Psalm 23:2 NIV).

Sounds like an idyllic hayride on the farm, doesn't it? It's a beautiful picture of God leading us to a place of rest and peace, but unfortunately, the journey doesn't end there. David goes on to say that at other times the ride takes us through the darkest valleys, the valley of the shadow of death, as the King James version calls it.

We've all been there. Sometimes life takes us down roads far more frightening than any artificial scares cooked up around Halloween. Whether it's a diagnosis at the doctor or bad news from your boss, divorce papers or a phone call in the middle of the night telling you that a loved one is gone, we know just how terrifying it can feel to walk through dark valleys.

Yet, even in these dark valleys, David said, "I will fear no evil" (Psalm 23:4 NIV). Why? Because God was with him. With him in the green pastures and with him in the shadows. And that made all the difference.

The great thing about hayrides is that we each get to choose which type we prefer, whether it's a tranquil ride in the country or the thrills of the scarier variety. If only we had such choices in the experiences of everyday life. Unfortunately, that part's out of our control.

The one choice we do get to make, however, is who we invite to join us on the journey.

Journal Prompts

What type of hayride do you prefer? Peaceful and serene or one that's full of surprises?

What's your life journey been like lately? Does it feel more like an idyllic ride on the farm or a trip through the darkest valley?

Have you ever experienced God's peace even in challenging circumstances? What helps you to experience God's presence?

God, thank you for walking with me
through the darkest valley.
Help to experience your peace wherever I go.

Amen

8

TRUE COLORS

For our present troubles are small and won't last very long.
Yet they produce for us a glory that vastly outweighs them
and will last forever!

– 2 CORINTHIANS 4:17 (NLT)

I love fall in the Smokies, not the hustle and bustle of the tourist traps, but the quiet of the mountains, where the trees are exploding with color. It starts in the higher elevations where streaks of orange and yellow and scarlet flow like lava to the valleys below.

On rainy days, the leaves are electric, like neon against iron skies. On sunny days, the slopes are blinding. It's hard to believe this much beauty begins with darkness, but that's the way it works.

See, it's not just the cool temperatures that ignite a tree's fall colors. It's also the long nights. Deciduous trees know when the days are growing shorter in autumn. They sense it in their bones. The darkness tells them to seal up their trunks and cut off the steady supply of chlorophyll they've been pumping into their leaves all summer long.[3]

As the green chlorophyll decays, the leaves reveal their true colors that have been hiding underneath. I didn't know this until recently, but leaves are born with yellow and orange pigments. You just can't see them under all that green.

It's only when the darkness comes, only when they begin to die, that their beauty is revealed.

In this dying season some leaves even produce a new color, a brilliant red. It comes from a pigment called anthocyanins.[4] You can drop that word at a party to impress your friends. It's a pigment made by sugar trapped in the leaves, another byproduct of the dying process.

This festival of decomposition puts on quite a show. Some people call it nature's fireworks. I call it a picture of the spiritual life.

In the darkest hours of our lives, our true colors are revealed, the character God has been cultivating in us all along. It's hard to see it in the green season, but in the dying season, when the things we rely on for our comfort and peace are stripped away, the beauty of our soul is unveiled.

This doesn't just apply to physical death, but to the everyday process of dying to ourselves, of choosing to walk away from old patterns of life to embrace all that God has for us and of trying to be faithful even when life throws pain and suffering our way.

The apostle Paul, a man familiar with suffering, said this hardship produces a new kind of beauty in us, our own spiritual anthocyanins glowing like fire in our hearts. He said, "For our present troubles are small and won't last very long. Yet they produce for us a glory that vastly outweighs them and will last forever" (2 Corinthians 4:17 NLT).

Paul experienced more pain than most of us ever will. Yet he considered it nothing compared to the reward that is waiting on the other side, the beauty of a transformed heart and the celebration of heaven that will make even the most spectacular fall leaves look dull by comparison.

After all, the Artist who paints every autumn with color is the same Artist who created you as his masterpiece. Someday you will see him face-to-face. He will say, "Well done, good and faithful servant," and the darkness will be no more.

Journal Prompts

Where is your favorite place to go to see the fall colors? What does this beauty tell you about God?

Have you ever seen someone demonstrate beautiful faith in difficult circumstances?

What true colors do you hope people will see in you the next time you face a trial?

God, you are the ultimate Artist.
Thank you for painting the amazing colors
of fall. I pray that you would help me to live
a beautiful life even on my darkest day.

Amen

9

SNEAK PREVIEW

He has planted eternity in the human heart.

– ECCLESIASTES 3:11 (NLT)

Back in my day, we couldn't watch new TV shows until the fall. We didn't have this Netflix nonsense, where you can binge-watch a whole season of a show at once, and the only entertainment we ever streamed was in the creek by my front yard.

Kids in my day had to learn patience. The annual television season was a real thing back then. It followed the school calendar like everything else in my life. That meant new shows premiered in the fall, wrapped up in the spring and then cycled through an endless sea of reruns all summer long.

By the time my friends and I made it back to school, we were salivating for new shows like parched castaways waiting for the new TV season to rescue us from our fate.

The herald of this rescue operation was the fall preview issue of the *TV Guide*. I'm not talking about that oversized magazine you see on newsstands today. I mean the old pocket-sized *TV Guide*, extra fat because of the special section previewing the new fall shows.

It was in this tome of wonders that I first beheld a talking Trans-Am, a team of mercenaries with a big guy sporting a mohawk, and a private investigator who drove around Hawaii in a cool, red Ferrari. Throughout the school year my friends and I would act out the adventures of *Knight Rider*, the *A-Team*, *Magnum PI* and other shows like them every chance we got, but it was in that fall preview issue that I got my first glimpse of the adventures that awaited us.

It's funny to think about how much time I spent looking forward to something that seems so silly as an adult. Yet, as human beings I think we all know we're made to be a part of a bigger adventure. The book of Ecclesiastes says that God "has planted eternity in the human heart" (3:11 NLT). In other words, deep down we know we're made for more.

As kids, we see this longing play out in the things we pretend to be. Whether fairy princesses or superheroes, sports stars or rock stars, every kid knows they're made for something extraordinary. Unfortunately, life has a way of pounding it out of them.

As adults we end up chasing other things to be extraordinary: a bigger house, a better job, another degree, a more attractive spouse, more likes on Facebook, or anything we can find to satisfy that eternal longing embedded in our hearts. Nothing is wrong with a bigger house, better job or more education, but we've all seen people pursue good things in an unhealthy way.

Maybe we've seen it in ourselves. I know I have.

But there's another way: two thousand years ago, one man gave us a sneak preview of a different kind of life, a life that finds satisfaction and significance in a deep relationship with God.

That man's name, of course, was Jesus. Jesus gave us a glimpse of what it looks like to live out the adventure we were made to live, a God-centered life poured out in the service of others. Jesus showed us what it looks like to have true joy, strength and peace.

And not only did he show us a preview of the adventure we were made to live, but by dying on the cross, he made it possible for us to jump into this epic story with God.

If you feel like your life is stuck in reruns, maybe it's time to change the channel. Check out the sneak preview of the life you could be living by taking a look a fresh look at Jesus and the adventure that may be waiting for you this fall.

Journal Prompts

Have you ever found yourself caught up in a story, whether it was a movie, TV show or a book? What was so appealing about it to you?

What is one of your favorite stories about Jesus? What do you love about it?

Imagine that the Jesus story you chose was a preview of your own life. What would it look like for you to live out that story today? What's one small way you could copy the life of Jesus?

God, thank you for Jesus.
Thank you for his example of an amazing life.
Please show me how I can imitate him today.

Amen

10

Amazing God

Trust in the Lord with all your heart;
do not depend on your own understanding.
Seek his will in all you do,
and he will show you which path to take.

– Proverbs 3:5-6 (NLT)

Several years ago I took my daughters to one of those fancy pumpkin patches that is half-family farm and half-Disneyland. It had a petting zoo, haunted house, hayride, and even a couple of corn mazes. I love corn mazes, so I refused to allow anyone to get their pumpkins until we went exploring. Just to make it interesting I let my girls take turns choosing which way to go.

We had a blast for the first five minutes or so. The maze was significantly larger than the one we had at our old pumpkin patch. We had plenty of places to make wrong turns and get completely lost which is, of course, the whole point of going into a maze.

My seven-year-old loved it, but my five-year-old grew anxious fast. The longer we spent in the maze the tighter she squeezed my hand. Her sister tried to get her to run off ahead with her, but she refused to leave my side. I tried to help her save face and said, "She just wants to stick with her dad because she's afraid she'll lose me."

My daughter, with a little panic in her voice, said, "No, I'm afraid I'll lose me!"

I know what she means. In the maze of life it's easy to lose ourselves. Every day we're faced with a gazillion choices, most of which aren't clearly labeled as right or wrong. Navigating this complicated world can be overwhelming and, at times, downright scary. Sometimes we end up taking paths that lead us to places we never thought we'd go.

That's why we all need a heavenly Dad who can hold our hand and keep us from getting lost. It's like the wise king Solomon once wrote, "Trust in the Lord with all your heart; do not depend on your own understanding. Seek his will in all you do, and he will show you which path to take" (Psalm 23:4 NIV).

I noticed that when choosing directions, my girls typically either followed the people in front of us or took the widest, most well-worn path. That's how we got lost.

As a grown-up, I had a better sense of direction. I knew which way we had to go, but it meant taking a tiny rabbit trail that no one thought was a good idea until it led us right out of the maze.

In the same way, as we follow God, sometimes he'll take us down paths that don't make much sense at the time, but if we trust him and cling to his hand we'll eventually find our way.

Journal Prompts

How do you feel when you're facing a tough choice?

Do you have a difficult choice to make right now? Have you prayed about it?

Who are some godly people who might be able to help you process this decision?

God, thanks for never leaving me.
Please remind me to turn to you when life gets confusing.
Show me how to follow you and make wise choices today.

Amen

11

LEAF COLLECTION

This is the message you have heard from the beginning:
We should love one another.

- 1 JOHN 3:11 (MSG)

I had two major problems helping my daughter put together her fall leaf collection for school. First, we only have three trees in our yard. Second, those are about the only trees I can identify, and that's because I planted them.

The way I figured it, she either needed a smarter dad or we needed to get some help. We didn't have time for the first option, so we had to get creative.

Fortunately we have a fantastic park in our town with a wide variety of trees, and they are all labeled with tiny signs. I have a suspicion the trees were planted to help kids like mine get a good grade on their leaf assignments no matter who their parents might be.

Labels are a fantastic resource. They can help you make sense out of things you don't understand. *Hmm, what is that tree with gigantic leaves? It's huge! Oh, it's a Bigleaf Magnolia.*

They can also help you differentiate between two things that are similar. *Hey, is that a Sugar Maple? Nope, it's a Red Maple. They kind of look alike.*

And labels make it easy to identify an object without having to carefully examine it each time. *How many lobes does that thing have? Do the veins go all the way to the edge? Who cares? Just read the sign!*

It's no wonder as humans we love to categorize and label things. It just makes life simpler. This is great when it comes to helping your kid with a fall leaf collection. Not so great when we try to apply the same principle to people.

People are hard to understand, especially people who are different than us—different personalities, different backgrounds, different political parties, different nationalities, different generations or different whatever. So to make life simpler, we just use labels.

Oh, you know how Maria is. She's such an introvert.

Ray? I can't stand that guy. He's one of those artistic types.

Don't get me started on Sarah. You know who she voted for.

It's convenient to label people but rarely accurate. Why? Because human beings are way more complicated than that. We all know that's true about ourselves. You ever had someone try to label you or lump you in with a stereotype?

We bristle against that kind of treatment because we know it's not fair. We're so much more than the labels other people try to hang on us, but sometimes we struggle remembering the same is true for others.

That's why Jesus gave the human race one big label. It says "beloved." Each of one us is treasured by God, and he expects us to treat each other accordingly.

Jesus said, "So now I am giving you a new commandment: Love each other. Just as I have loved you, you should love each other" (John 13:34 NLT).

Last month I visited that same park again where we found the labels on all the trees. They were hosting an art fair, and the sidewalks were jammed with people checking out the booths that lined both sides. There were paintings, wood carvings, sculptures, leather crafts and every other artistic medium you could imagine. The crowd was just as eclectic as the artwork in the booths, people of every shape, size, color, clothing style and walk of life.

It would have been so easy for me to label each one of them and for them to label me.

But that's when it hit me, just a beautiful thought out of the blue. The real works of art here aren't in the booths. They're on the sidewalk in front of me. Masterpiece creations all made in the image of God. For just a second I caught a glimpse of how spectacular, how fantastic, everyone in the crowd must look to him.

No one wonder Jesus told us to love beyond labels. He saw people as they truly are. I hope as I follow him, I can learn to do the same.

So this fall, let's save our labels for leaf collections and other projects where we're sure to need their help. When it comes to dealing with people, however, let's stick to the label of love.

Journal Prompts

Have you ever had someone label you, misjudge you or limit you to a stereotype? How did that make you feel?

Do you ever struggle to relate to people who are different than you? How can you try to get to know them better so that you can see them like Jesus does?

Who's the hardest person for you to love right now? What's one practical way you can show them God's love?

God, thank you for showing me what love really is.
Help me to see other people the way you see them
and to love everyone the way you love them.

Amen

12

WHAT ARE YOU GOING TO BE?

For we are God's masterpiece.
He has created us anew in Christ Jesus,
so we can do the good things he planned for us long ago.

– EPHESIANS 2:10 (NLT)

It was never about the candy. Never. Candy was just an excuse. It gave us a reason to trick-or-treat. Never once, though, did another kid ask me, "What kind of chocolate are you going to get this year?"

Instead, we asked the other question, the magic question. What are you going to be this year? Not, what are you going to wear? What are you going to be?

When we were kids, we didn't just put on costumes. We took on new identities. We transformed, and every October the possibilities were endless.

I became Superman, Batman, and Darth Vader, among others. I didn't just walk from house to house. I flew. I swung. I zoomed across town in the Batmobile. For a night, I wasn't just a chubby kid with homework and glasses. I was whatever I wanted to be. Heroic. Powerful. Awesome.

Afterwards, it didn't matter that I had to go back to being my normal old self for the next eleven months. I had a bucket full of candy as a consolation prize, and Christmas was just around the corner. But more than that, I knew October would eventually come around again, and the stores would restock their shelves with those costume boxes, the ones with the plastic windows on the lids that served as gateways to another world.

Once more my friends and I would ask the question: What are you going to be?

At some point, though, I stopped believing in the magic of masks and vinyl suits. Unfortunately, it wasn't just that I gave up the childhood fantasy of Halloween, but in the underlying truth that made it so powerful.

I stopped believing in the miracle of transformation. I stopped believing I could become something other than what I am today.

How about you? Did you have big dreams as a kid, but now those dreams don't seem possible? Are there areas of your life you wish you could change, but don't believe you can?

I'll never lose this weight. I'll never get out of debt. I'll never have the courage to say no. I'll never start my own business. I'll never escape my past. I'll never kick this addiction. I'll never forgive him. I'll never make this marriage work. I'll never amount to anything. I'll never get my act together. I'll never be happy.

The word "never" is a padlock on our future. It says I am this and not that, and nothing will ever change it. But the good news is there is a God who holds the key to that lock. He is the God of possibilities who blows away our "nevers" like a house of cards.

Just ask David, a back-woods shepherd boy whom God turned into a king. Or Zacchaeus, a crook who became the most generous man in town. Or Peter, a lying coward transformed into a hero of faith.

Paul, a guy who had his own life turned upside-down by God, explains it like this, "God can do anything, you know—far more than you could ever imagine or guess or request in your wildest dreams! He does it not by pushing us around but by working within us, his Spirit deeply and gently within us" (Ephesians 3:20 MSG).

When it comes to your future, God doesn't believe in never. He believes in you. He's still young enough and playful enough to believe in the miracle of transformation and that you can become anything he wants you to be.

So wherever you feel stuck, whatever seems impossible to change, turn it over to him. He's waiting like a kid on Halloween to ask you that magic question. What are you going to be this year? What are you going to be?

Journal Prompts

What is one thing that seems impossible for you to change about yourself? Have you given up hope of ever changing? Why?

How can you invite God into the process? What is one step you could take to surrender this area to him?

What dreams do you think God might have for your life? What's holding you back from becoming the person God made you to be?

God, you can do anything. Nothing is impossible for you.
I know I can become anything you want me to be.
Please help me to never give up on your dreams for me.

Amen

13

You're Never Too Old

But grow in the grace and knowledge
of our Lord and Savior Jesus Christ.

2 Peter 3:18 (NLT)

One of the worst moments of childhood is the day you realize you're too old to trick-or-treat. It creeps up on you subtly. One year you're scared the big kids are going to take your candy. The next year you notice nobody is bigger than you.

At school, you're afraid to bring it up. Some of your friends are talking about going out and playing pranks. Others are making fun of the kids who are buying costumes. Still, there's the silent majority who don't know what to do. Sure, you're growing up, but who wants to give up all that free candy? Who wants to miss out on masks and colored hairspray and the cool stuff that goes with it?

If only the government would set a legal limit, things would be simpler. We have an age for driving, an age for drinking, even an age for retirement. Would it kill Congress to establish a trick-or-treating age and put all the confused tweens out of their misery?

If you or someone you love is in the midst of this dilemma, let me offer some help. Here are seven tips to help you know when you might be too old for trick-or-treating:

1. Every time you say "trick-or-treat," your voice cracks.
2. You drive yourself from house to house.
3. You decide to save money by wearing your prom dress.
4. Your *Duck Dynasty* costume doesn't require a fake beard.
5. You invite your fraternity brothers to go with you.
6. Your wife makes you share any chocolate you get with her.
7. You're dressed as your favorite Bee Gee.

If any of those describe you, maybe it's time to rethink your Halloween plans.

Eventually most of us make the transition from taking candy to giving it away. It's all part of growing up. Or, at least, it's supposed to be. But then again, sometimes we don't always outgrow the things we should.

You ever do something just to impress your friends? That's understandable in middle school, but a different story when you're middle-aged. Have you ever bent the truth to avoid a tough conversation? That's one thing when you're four, but another matter when you're 34. Ever jealous when your friends get new toys? Pout when you don't get your way?

Well, you get the picture. Some of us may be too old for trick-or-treating, but unfortunately, we're never too old to act immature.

On the plus side, though, we're never too old to start growing up. The Bible is full of gray-haired graduates of the school of spiritual growth. Moses was 80 years old when God helped him overcome his fear. Abraham was over 100 when God taught him how to trust in his promises. And Zechariah was simply described as "very old" when he learned how to keep his mouth shut and listen to God (Luke 1:7 NIV).

That means there's hope for any of us who are ready to hang up our candy buckets and ask God to help us take a step towards maturity today.

Journal Prompts

Did you go trick-or-treating as a kid? How did you know when you were old enough to give it up?

What's one area of your life God has helped you to grow in over the years?

Where do you think God may be calling you to do a little growing up today? Who is someone who could encourage you in this process?

God, thank you for helping me to grow up in my faith. Please show me where I need to take a step toward maturity and give me the strength to do it.

Amen

14

THE MARK OF ZORRO

I praise you because I am fearfully and wonderfully made;
your works are wonderful. I know that full well.

- PSALM 139:14 (NIV)

When I was in third grade, I thought I had the coolest Halloween costume on the planet. Every year before this, we'd bought my costume from the store, but this year was going to be different. I wanted to be something that didn't come from a box. I wanted to be Zorro.

Zorro was basically Batman on a horse. He didn't have a utility belt or fancy gadgets. He didn't need them. He had a black stallion, a sword and plenty of attitude to back them up.

I didn't have a horse, so I needed the costume to make up for it. Unfortunately, all I had was a black tracksuit with a thin white stripe down the pants legs and a colorful emblem on the jacket. It would have to do.

My mom helped me out by dying an old bed sheet black for the cape, and my dad spray-painted a straw cowboy hat to match. It was a little more in the style of the Marlboro Man than Zorro but I didn't care. I thought it was awesome.

When I marched into my elementary school Halloween party, I felt like the most dangerous Zorro the world had ever seen. For about five minutes.

Then, I saw the other Zorro. He was a fifth grader, and his costume was dead on. Spanish gaucho hat. No dumb white stripes on his pants. Even his plastic sword was cooler than mine. I went from hero to zero in a heartbeat.

There was no use pretending. I was a second rate Zorro, and everyone knew it.

You ever feel like that? Your day is going great until you run into someone younger, thinner or cuter. Suddenly you feel like a leftover. You love your new job until your friend tells you about his. Now yours doesn't sound so hot. Your car, your spouse and your kids all look worse when compared with the fifth-grade Zorros of the world.

Comparing your life to others always magnifies your flaws. It distorts reality, masks the good, and robs you of gratitude and joy.

Maybe that's why the Bible is so big on contentment. It talks about discovering the secret of being content in each and every situation. That secret is believing that our worth, our identity and our provision comes from the hand of a God who loves us. When we anchor our lives into that bedrock, we give up the comparison game.

It frees us to enjoy being who God made us to be, white striped pants and all.

You know, not long after the Halloween party, I forgot all about that other Zorro. I didn't have time to dwell on it. I had work to do. I'm proud to say that not a single trick-or-treater got attacked by outlaws that night thanks to me. I guess that's what happens when you stop worrying about how you stack up next to the other guy and just get down to the business of being yourself.

Journal Prompts

Do you ever struggle with comparing yourself to others? In what ways?

The Bible says that God made you in a unique and special way. What are three things that make you unique? If you're having trouble thinking of them, ask a trusted friend.

Who can you encourage today in their uniqueness? Give them a call or send them a text and let them know one thing you appreciate about them.

> *God, thank you for making me as your special creation.*
> *Please help me to not compare myself to others,*
> *but to be content with who I am and*
> *comfortable in my own skin.*
>
> *Amen*

15

TRICK-OR-TREAT REPEAT

This means that anyone who belongs to Christ has become
a new person. The old life is gone; a new life has begun!

– 2 CORINTHIANS 5:17 (NLT)

No one told me I was supposed to wear pants. Not my mom. Not my dad. Not any of the neighborhood kids I went trick-or-treating with that night. No one.

See, this is what happens when you put fathers in charge of getting kids ready. My mom had to work late that night, and it was up to my dad to get me in my costume before she got home. How hard could that be?

He apparently thought the same thing and just handed me the costume box and walked away. No instructions. No questions about my ability to dress myself correctly. And certainly no warnings about the inherent dangers of wearing cheap, plastic costumes without real clothes on underneath.

I guess some things you have to learn the hard way.

But what did I know? It was the fall of 1979. I was seven-years-old and desperate to get out the door and start raking in the candy. So I did what I thought I was supposed to do, stripped down to my underwear, threw on that flimsy, vinyl costume and headed out the door.

When my mom arrived, she had no clue. She was just excited that my dad and I had actually managed to get ready without her help. Boy, was she wrong. I was a ticking time bomb about to embarrass myself in front of the entire neighborhood.

Everything started off fine. We gathered up several friends who lived on my street and started going door-to-door. I picked up a few Tootsie Rolls and some gum, and then the good stuff started rolling in. SweeTarts, Hershey Miniatures, that sort of thing.

And then it happened. Don't ask me why. In all my years of trick-or-treating with those paper thin costumes, in all those years when I had pants on underneath, it had never happened. Not once. Not even close.

But this year, the one and only year I was underdressed, it did happen. Yes, you guessed it. My costume ripped. Right up the inseam of one leg and right down the other.

"Uh, mom," I said.

She gasped when she saw me; gasped, I tell you. Her eyes were as big as pumpkins and her face as white as my briefs.

"Why aren't you wearing pants?" she screamed.

"Pants?" I said. "No one said anything about pants!"

At that point, the sheer horror of the moment crashed over me like a tsunami. Here I was in the middle of our small town, surrounded by my neighborhood friends in my underwear.

What had started as the greatest night of that season had turned into the worst. Without a doubt Halloween was ruined, and I would be too ashamed to leave the house for the next hundred years.

But then my mom did the impossible. She turned the worst into the best. She took me home, threw together a homemade costume from junk she found in my closet and took me right back out trick-or-treating.

And best of all, she let me hit the same houses I had already visited! After all, no one would recognize me in my new disguise. I felt like I was getting away with the crime of the century.

One thing I learned that night is that no failure is final. No matter how devastating our circumstances may seem, there's always an opportunity for a fresh start. I learned that lesson from my mom, but over the years have learned it time and time again in my relationship with God.

Even in our most embarrassing moments, even in our deepest shame, there is a God who can do the impossible. He can turn our worst into our best. He is an expert at new beginnings and second chances.

There are days when our best-laid plans tear at the seams like chintzy Halloween vinyl, days when we're shamed by our own foolishness, days when we think we're just done.

Those are the days when God is waiting to pick us up, repair the damage and put us back in the game, and, just like the Halloween of 1979, we will discover on those days that the second time around is always better than the one before.

Journal Prompts

Have you ever embarrassed yourself and wished you could have a do-over? Are there any mistakes from your past you keep replaying in your head?

What lies are you believing about yourself based on your past? Write them down, release them to God and rip up the list.

Where do you need to make a fresh start today?

God, you are the God of second chances.
I pray that you would wipe away the mistakes I've made
in the past and help me start over with you today.

Amen

16

SCARECROW

This is my command—be strong and courageous! Do not be afraid or discouraged. For the Lord your God is with you wherever you go.

– JOSHUA 1:9 (NLT)

My dog hates scarecrows. Despises them. Last year I brought one home to put up by our front porch, and it drove her nuts. She thought it was a real person, an intruder lurking on her doorstep who was up to no good.

She barked. She growled. She pawed at the glass. She wanted to tear it to pieces. I thought she was going to crash right through the door to get it.

Eventually I had to take down the scarecrow and throw it away. It was the only way to make peace with my pooch.

I'm not one to judge, though. At times we all get worked up over things that don't really matter.

When I was three, my parents let me a watch a movie that featured menacing tree monsters. I got so scared that I jumped to my feet, ran to the TV and started pounding the screen. The tree monsters never stood a chance.

Fear can make us do funny things. Sometimes we go on the

attack, lashing out because we're afraid. Heaven help anyone who gets in our way.

Other times we just run and hide. We may avoid the subject of our fear or even lie to keep from having to deal with it.

Then there are times when fear simply paralyzes us. We don't fight. We don't hide. We just freeze. We find it hard to even function because we are terrified.

There is a great story in the Bible about a king named Jehoshaphat who had plenty of reasons to be afraid. He got word that an enormous army was coming to conquer his people. His nation was so outnumbered that they didn't stand a chance. So Jehoshaphat got everyone together, fasted, prayed, and asked God what to do.

God said, "Do not be afraid or discouraged because of this vast army. For the battle is not yours, but God's . . . You will not have to fight this battle" (2 Chronicles 20:15, 17 NIV).

Whew! I bet that was a relief to hear, but here's the interesting thing. God still had them march to the battlefield. Yes, God promised to handle it, but he still made Jehoshaphat face his fear. Why? Because that's where trust is born.

It's one thing to say we trust God when we're hiding in the closet. It's another thing to say it when we're marching off to war. But Jehoshaphat and his people chose the way of trust. By the time they arrived at the battlefield, the vast army that had terrorized them had already been defeated. The fight was over before it had even begun.

It always is with God.

Some of the fears we face are completely legitimate. Others, not so much. But when we're in the middle of it, it's hard to know which is which. So when your fear shows up like a scarecrow taunting you at the door, just relax and remember the one who fights for you. When we stack our fears up against him, it's no contest at all.

Journal Prompts

How do you typically react to fear? Do you tend to go on the attack, hide or just freeze up? What would it look like to take your fear to God instead?

What are you afraid of right now? How does fear keep you from experiencing the life God has for you?

Make a list of things your fear can do versus the things God can do. Which one is bigger?

God, you are bigger than all my fears.
Help me to focus on you today. I don't want to miss out
on the life you have for me. I want to live a life of courage
because you are with me wherever I go.

Amen

17

THANK YOU, THING

For my thoughts are not your thoughts,
neither are your ways my ways.

– ISAIAH 55:8 (NIV)

When I was a kid, I wanted to live with the Addams family. As an only child who was raised in the days of three-channel television, you think about these things. Sure, the Brady house was fun, and *The Beverly Hillbillies* had an awesome pool, but the Addams' mansion was a boy's dream world.

Where else could you have sword fights in the living room and blow up your train set in the attic? There were no carnivorous plants in Lucy and Ricky's apartment, and no lions roaming around Andy Taylor's house in Mayberry. But the Addams family had it all. Though they may have been creepy, kooky, mysterious and spooky, Gomez and Morticia had the coolest TV house in sitcom history.

And my absolute favorite part? Thing. Who wouldn't want to have their own Thing?

In case you're unfamiliar with the show, Thing was the disembodied hand who was one of the Addams family's most faithful servants. Whenever they needed him, Thing would pop out of his box and be ready to serve at a moment's notice. Thing delivered the mail, lit Gomez's cigars, and performed all kinds of helpful tasks for the family. Then he would disappear back in his box until someone needed him again.

Not that the Addams clan didn't appreciate it. In fact the most memorable line from the show has to be the courteous catchphrase used by nearly every member of the family, "Thank you, Thing."

As I grew up, I gave up my dream of living like an Addams, but I suppose deep down I never lost my desire to have a servant like Thing.

Maybe that's why I sometimes treat God the way I do. I call on him when I need him, politely thank him when he blesses me, and then hope he goes back in his box until I need him again. It's an appealing fantasy to believe that I could have God as my servant, a cosmic hand always available at my beck and call.

Thank you, God. Now, go back in your box.

It doesn't take much life experience to realize that's just a fantasy. God's not my servant, not my genie and not my cosmic vending machine. He is not my Thing. But he does want to have a relationship with me, not as my butler, but as my King and my Dad.

God cannot be kept in a box that I open when I step into church or when I need a helping hand. And that's good news. In fact, it's the best news ever, because that means I'm not in charge. I don't have to figure everything out. I don't have to run my corner of the universe. God can handle that on his own, but he invites me into what he's doing in the world because he loves me and wants to share his life with me.

That means sometimes my prayers go unanswered. Sometimes I get a flat out "no." It means bad things still happen to me. It also means that sometimes God seems very active in my life and other times I wonder if he's even there, but that's how it goes relating to a God who won't stay in a box.

Maybe that's why God told his people, "For my thoughts are not your thoughts, neither are your ways my ways" (Isaiah 55:8 NIV).

That's where faith comes in, realizing that God's not a Thing, but a real, living being who, though a bit confusing, surprising, unpredictable even, can always be trusted to do what's right.

And for that I say, "Thank you, God. Thank you."

Journal Prompts

Do you treat God more like a King or a Thing? Do you only go to him with your requests or do you ask him what he wants of you?

Are there any circumstances in your life where you need to remember that God is in control?

Are there any areas of your life that have been off limits to God? Is there anything you need to surrender to him today?

God, you are the King of the universe. I am your creation, and I release control of my life to you. I am here to love you and serve you with all my heart.

Amen

18

FINDING THE PERFECT PUMPKIN

You didn't choose me. I chose you.

– JOHN 15:16 (NLT)

When you have kids, finding the perfect pumpkin is easier said than done. Every October, I drive my family out to our favorite pumpkin patch in a quest for the holy grail of Halloween fruit.

This was a huge production when my kids were preschoolers. We had to pack snacks and drinks and make sure everyone took a potty break before we hiked from the parking lot to the pumpkin patch located somewhere near the South American border. Okay, maybe it wasn't quite in South America, but, trust me, it was a long haul, especially with two little ones in tow.

Once we made it to the pumpkin patch, however, the real work began. Somehow we had to navigate the sea of orange and green to find the one, perfect pumpkin. There were hundreds of choices, and my kids wanted to examine every single one. Twice.

To make matters more complicated, their definition of perfect was slightly different than mine. When it came to pumpkins, my daughters' love was blind. They didn't care if it was rotting on the ground or green on the vine.

Warts? No problem. Discolored? Not an issue. A huge gouge cleaving the pumpkin in two? What gouge?

If there were an island of misfit pumpkins, my daughters would take them all. Despite my efforts to steer them to the classic round, orange and smooth variety, they tend to follow their hearts.

In that way, they reflect the heart of God.

A follower of Jesus named Paul once wrote, "Even before he made the world, God loved us and chose us . . . This is what he wanted to do, and it gave him great pleasure" (Ephesians 1:4-5, NLT).

You would think as God looked over the vines of humanity entangled throughout history, he would have a wealth of great options when picking those to join his family. The keenest of minds. The purest of hearts. The most courageous of leaders. He could choose the popular, the beautiful, the perfect.

But that's the weird thing about God. He picks everybody. Warts and all. Feel like a loser? No problem. Got a shady past? Not an issue. Made some mistakes? What mistakes?

Whether you shine like a jack o' lantern or act like a pumpkin head, you are loved and chosen. God. Picks. You. Even when no one else does. Especially when no one else does.

God's love isn't blind, but it is big, big enough for you and me. All God asks in return is for us to embrace that truth and to live a life that flows out of that deep place of love and acceptance.

As for me, it's getting easier to believe. I watch it play out every year in a vast pumpkin patch somewhere near the South American border. It always ends the same. I finally realize that the perfect pumpkin is whichever one my girls pick. Their love bestows a value of its own. I'm thankful for a love like that. I'm thankful for being picked.

Journal Prompts

Have you ever felt overlooked or rejected? When?

How does it make you feel to realize that you are chosen by God?

What would change in your life if you really believed you are unconditionally loved and accepted?

God, thank you for choosing me. Help me to stop trying to earn your love or the approval of man. I want to live like I'm loved and share that love with others today.

Amen

19

HALLOWEEN SCROOGE

God loves a cheerful giver.

– 2 CORINTHIANS 9:7 (NIV)

YYou can tell a lot about a person by what they give out on Halloween. Take the guy I met in the big, brick house, for instance.

Several years ago, I took my oldest daughter trick-or-treating in a nice neighborhood with some friends. The houses there don't come cheap. Like half-a-million-dollars not cheap.

You would think you'd get the best candy at a place like that, like it should be a part of the homeowner association dues. But Brick House Guy didn't get that memo.

When one of our kids rang his doorbell, the guy came out and said to our whole group of trick-or-treaters, "I'm not giving out candy." Then he closed his garage door, turned out his porch light and went back inside.

Turns out not all Scrooges show up at Christmas. You can be a tightwad any time of year.

On the other extreme, there are my next-door neighbors. Do

you know what they gave my kids two years ago? A five-pound Hershey chocolate bar.

That's right. I said five pounds.

That's 80 ounces. 2,268 grams. We're talking the equivalent of 162 Hershey miniatures or 52 full-size candy bars.

Two years later my kids were still bouncing off the walls.

A five-pound chocolate bar is ridiculously generous, which is just what God calls us to be.

It reminds me of a story in the Bible when Jesus was having dinner with some friends. The friends included a man named Lazarus, who not long before was rotting in a tomb. Jesus changed that.

To show her gratitude, Lazarus' sister, Mary, came in with a jar of perfume. We're not talking Wal-Mart's Britney Spears collection. We're not even talking Chanel No. 5. This jar cost a year's salary.

Mary broke the jar and poured the whole thing out on Jesus' feet as an act of love. A year's salary. If it had been a Hershey bar, it would have been around 5,000–8,000 pounds.

But Mary just gave it away.

What I learn from people like that is that your bank account and your zip code do not determine your level of generosity. Gratitude does.

Mary was ridiculously grateful and that made her ridiculously generous. Brick house or poor house, giving overflows from your heart.

Sometimes we think if we made more money we would give more of it away. Not true. If we had more gratitude, then we'd give more away. Being thankful for what God's given us transforms us into five pound Hershey bar kind of people.

But when we're ungrateful, when we feel entitled, when we focus on what we don't have, we slam the door of our hearts like Brick House Guy slammed his front door on a bunch of cute trick-or-treaters.

Jesus said it like this, "For where your treasure is, there your heart will be also" (Matt 6:21 NIV).

How much candy we give away this Halloween probably doesn't matter much, but it's not a bad place to start.

Journal Prompts

Do you tend to focus more on enjoying what you have or worrying about what you don't have?

What are five things you are grateful for today? Make a list and put it somewhere you can see it regularly.

What is one way you could practice generosity this week?

God, thank for all you have given me. You are a ridiculously generous God. Help me to have a thankful heart so I can be free to live generously today.

Amen

20

Better Late Than Never

It's not important who does the planting or who does the watering.
What's important is that God makes the seed grow.

– 1 Corinthians 3:7 (NLT)

Last fall, I had a yard full of pumpkin vines but no pumpkins in sight. My daughter wanted to plant them in the spring, but we got them out so late that we knew it was a race against the clock. The vines were sprawling. They invaded a good-sized chunk of our backyard but didn't look like they were doing much more than killing the grass.

However, I am an optimist at heart, and I love my kids, so I let it go through October. By the day before Halloween, though, I thought it was time to give up the ghost, so to speak. If the vines hadn't produced anything by now, it was game over.

My daughter was disappointed to say the least. She'd put all that time into planting, watering and checking on them for months, and by October she was emotionally invested.

I had to explain to her that it just wasn't in the cards. We'd have to try again next year.

Imagine my surprise, then, when I went out to chop down the

vine and discovered the cutest little pumpkin you've ever seen hiding under the canopy of leaves.

My daughter was ecstatic. We picked the pumpkin, cleaned it up and prominently displayed it on our front porch for all of our neighbors to see.

The growing process is funny like that. You may get a late start. You may not see much happening, and then, out of the blue, something springs to life.

It happens in our backyards and sometimes even in our own hearts. That's why our spiritual growth can be the most frustrating process in the world. It's easy to get excited in the planting season when your faith is new or you feel like God is breathing fresh truth into your life.

This time everything's going to be different, you think. This time you're going to make some changes. And you try.

You pray. You read your Bible. Maybe you even go to church and do whatever you can think of to cultivate this new spiritual life that's growing in your soul.

Then comes the waiting. Not much seems to be happening. Maybe like my family's pumpkin patch, you got a late start. You may even be like I was, ready to chop down the vine and give up altogether.

But what's easy to forget is that underneath the surface is where the real growth happens. God only knows how much progress we're actually making, or rather that he is making in us, until one day, out of the blue, it blossoms, and bears fruit in the most unexpected places.

Galatians 5 gives us a whole list of things like love, joy, peace, and patience that God may be growing in our lives right now even if we can't yet see the change. But that's okay. The Bible calls it the fruit of the Spirit, not the fruit of self-improvement or gritty determination or instant success. He is the one doing the growing. We are simply cooperating in the process.

So when you feel discouraged that you're not making much progress in your spiritual life, remember my daughter's last minute pumpkin harvest and remember that growth in the pumpkin patch and in the Spirit can be hard to measure.

Journal Prompts

What season of faith are you in right now? The planting season where everything is new and fresh? The harvest season where you're seeing real change? Or the growing season where you may not see much progress?

Have you ever found yourself thinking, "I'll never change?" What do you think God would have to say about that thought?

Think back over the past year or five years or ten. What is one area where God has helped you grow?

God, you are the source of life.
Thank you for changing me from the inside out.
Help me to be patient with you and myself
as you help me to grow to be like you.

Amen

21

CANDY LAND

Forget the former things; do not dwell on the past.
See, I am doing a new thing!

– ISAIAH 43:18-19 (NIV)

Every November I think about renting a portable storage unit for our leftover Halloween candy. My kids bring home sugar by the truckload. They're super cute so I suspect people give them more candy than other kids. Whatever the reason, they rake in more loot than a couple of card sharks after a weekend in Vegas. It's a load of fun Halloween night, but the stuff sits around forever.

We generally give our kids a 48-hour, post-Halloween sugar binge to make the biggest dent in the candy supply as possible.

By the 48-hour mark, though, they're swinging from the ceiling fans and shaving the cat so we have to cut them off. From there on out we pull in the reins and only let them have one piece of candy a day which means we'll have candy coming out our ears for months.

That's where I come in. Like any loving father, I take one for the team. Well, more than one. Unfortunately, after my own 48-hour candy binge (okay, maybe 72) my wife cuts me off as well. The ceiling fan just won't support my weight like it used to.

At that point, we're stuck. We have a stockpile of perfectly good candy just sitting around taking up valuable real estate in our tiny house. By Thanksgiving my wife is begging me to let her throw it away.

"You can't throw it away," I tell her. "Our kids worked hard for that candy. They love that candy. There are people starving around the world for goodness' sake. You can't go around throwing away perfectly good candy."

It's not that I'm actually going to send the candy to a third world country, but it's the principle of the matter. The candy doesn't even sound good anymore. I just hate to throw it away.

Thanks to me, we usually end up with a tub of candy that no one wants to eat stuffed in the back of our pantry until sometime around Easter. Then it mysteriously vanishes one day while I'm at work. I suspect the Easter Bunny has something to do with it.

I suppose we all hang on to some things longer than we should. Some of us are candy hoarders. Others of us hoard our clothes, knick-knacks or random junk.

Still there are others of us who are hoarders of the heart. We squirrel away all kinds of things in the deep places of our soul that no one sees.

Whether it's old wounds, old flames, or old failures, it's just plain old. Our hearts don't have enough room to hold all of those grudges, regrets, or might-have-beens. Like my leftover candy, there comes a time to just let it go.

Why? Because we are created by a God who is infinitely more concerned with our future than our past. He is a God who has bigger dreams for our lives than we could ever have on our own.

God promises that at the end of time he will make all things new, but that process has already begun. Sometimes the only thing that stands in the way of receiving the fresh life God wants to give us is us.

Halloween candy may taste great in October, but by November and December, I'd rather go for pie. In the same way, we will never be able to enjoy the new life God has in store for us as long as we hold on to the past.

Journal Prompts

Are you more of a hoarder or a cleaner? Do you tend to hold onto things longer than others?

Has your past ever held you back from enjoying the present?

Are you holding on to anything in your heart that you need to let go?

God, thank you for setting me free from my past. Show me anything I need to release to you today. I want to walk in freedom and enjoy the future you have for me.

Amen

22

THE BONUS HOUR

What you ought to say is, "If the Lord wants us to,
we will live and do this or that."
– JAMES 4:15 (NLT)

The best hour of every year is the bonus hour, the extra hour we get each fall when we set our clocks back to standard time. It may not be a big deal to you, but I've served as a pastor for over twenty years. That puts me up at the crack of dawn most Sunday mornings. On the week we "fall back," however, I have a bonus hour in my day.

What do I do with my bonus hour? Anything I want! It's the one hour of the year I'm pretty much guaranteed to have completely to myself.

My internal clock knows it's all a lie so I still wake up at the same time, but I have an extra hour that Sunday morning to read, pray, workout, whatever I want to do. It's like a tiny vacation in the middle of a busy season of life.

Of course, I have to pay for it in the spring. When we "spring forward" to daylight saving time six months later, the bill comes due, and I have to sacrifice an hour to even things out. It's worth it, though, because when the bonus hour arrives, it feels like a gift from heaven, sixty minutes of space to catch my breath and just enjoy being alive.

Wouldn't it be great to have a bonus hour every day? In a way, we actually do. If you think about it, life is unpredictable. None of us are guaranteed another minute of breath. That means that really each hour, every day is a bonus hour.

It's easy to kid ourselves, thinking that our lives will stretch out as an endless series of days, but every funeral we attend reminds us of the truth. We have absolutely no clue how much time God has given us.

The apostle James says it like this, "How do you know what your life will be like tomorrow? Your life is like the morning fog—it's here a little while, then it's gone. What you ought to say is, "If the Lord wants us to, we will live and do this or that" (James 4:14-15 NLT).

Not only is James saying that life is unpredictable. He's also saying that we have exactly the amount of time to do whatever God has put us on earth to do. Even in a world broken by sin, where death is temporarily a part of the equation, God is still the Lord of time. That means that every hour we do have is a gift from him.

Ephesians 5:16-17 reminds us, "So be careful how you live. Don't live like fools, but like those who are wise. Make the most of every opportunity in these evil days" (NLT).

In other words, make each hour your bonus hour and milk it for all it's worth by loving God and loving others every chance you get. That's what wise living looks like no matter how many hours you may or may not have.

When we "fall back" this year, let's take that extra hour to remember how every moment is a gift from God and consider how we can spend more time enjoying him and sharing that joy with others.

Journal Prompts

What would you do with an extra hour in your day?

If you knew you only had one hour left to live, how would you spend that time? Does your daily life reflect the same priorities?

What's one thing that would help you to be more present in each moment you have?

God, thank you for every moment you give me.
Help to me to see each hour as a gift
to be used for you and enjoyed with you.

Amen

23

HOLIDAY SWITCHEROO

Enter his gates with thanksgiving; go into his courts with praise.
Give thanks to him and praise his name.

– PSALM 100:4 (NIV)

Well, here we are again, almost to the third week of November, and all we see is Christmas, Christmas, Christmas. It's the same old story. The moment the Halloween masks disappear off the store shelves, they're replaced by Christmas trees and wrapping paper. Ironically, Thanksgiving gets nothing but leftovers. This poor holiday doesn't even have its own songs and movies. Thanksgiving is nothing more than a speed bump on the way to Santa and "Silent Night."

Don't get me wrong. I love Christmas, but if Thanksgiving were a pet, we'd all get turned in for neglect.

I say it's time to change all that. It's time to pull a little Robin Hood action and take from the rich and give to the poor. It's time for the redistribution of some major holiday wealth.

I'm proposing that we simply take a few songs and movies from Christmas and give them to Thanksgiving. It's not like Christmas will miss them. It has plenty.

Here's what it would look like. Instead of "Deck the Halls," we'll sing "Deck the Fall." "The Little Drummer Boy" will become "The Little Drumstick Boy." And, of course, "O Christmas Tree" will become "O Cranberry."

See what I mean? It's easy!

The movies would be even better. Who wouldn't want to watch these beloved holiday classics? First up is *A Thanksgiving Carol,* the story of a grumpy vegetarian who is visited by three ghostly pilgrims and encouraged to eat poultry. After that, we'd have *Frosty the Canned Yam,* a wonderful cartoon about a lovable yam who comes to life when topped with magic marshmallows. Finally, you won't want to miss *It's a Wonderful Wife,* a movie about an angel who visits The Pioneer Woman's husband and shows him how terrible his Thanksgiving dinner would be if he had married someone else.

Hopefully by now you can see how my fair and balanced approach to holiday media would give Thanksgiving the attention it truly deserves. But if none of this comes to pass, I guess that's okay too, because you don't need movies and songs to be truly thankful to God for all he's given you. In fact, you don't even need a holiday, just a simple prayer to give credit to the one who provides for us all.

The best thing about Thanksgiving is that it's an anytime, anywhere kind of thing. In fact, you can even start today. Thanksgiving is always just one prayer away.

Journal Prompts

Is Thanksgiving an important holiday for your family or more of a speed bump on the way to Christmas? What's your favorite part about each holiday?

What's one way you could make thankfulness more of a part of your everyday life?

What are you thankful for today? Have you taken the time to stop and tell God how much you appreciate what he's done?

God, you've done so much for me.
I don't need a holiday to tell you thanks, but I am
grateful for Thanksgiving as an excuse to just stop and
think about how good you have been to me.

Amen

24

SMELLS LIKE HOME

Jesus replied, "I am the bread of life.
Whoever comes to me will never be hungry again."

– JOHN 6:35 (NLT)

I've never smelled anything better than my great-grandmother's kitchen on Thanksgiving morning. She made yeast rolls from scratch–light, feathery rolls that dissolved on your tongue like cotton candy.

My grandparents hosted Thanksgiving dinner at their house just across the street, and my favorite job was going to my great-grandmother's to help her carry over the rolls. The minute you opened her front door, it smelled like heaven. It made you forget every other food you'd ever eaten.

Turkey? Cranberry? Apple pie? Who needs them? As soon as I smelled those rolls, I had a one-track mind.

The warmth of that kitchen was so inviting on those chilly November mornings that it made me just want to go in, sit down with those rolls and never leave.

It had been over thirty years since I'd smelled my great-grandmother's cooking or anything like it. Then, on the Monday before

Thanksgiving last year, I walked into a grocery store bakery of all places, and the aroma hit me. Yeast rolls. It took me instantly back to that cozy kitchen on Thanksgiving morning where all was right in the world.

It was the smell of home.

My experience was nothing new. God's been using bread to remind people of good things for thousands of years. Take the Israelites, for example. God told them to bake unleavened bread to remember the Passover, the night he rescued them from slavery in Egypt. Later, God gave the same people a mysterious bread called manna to sustain them on their way to their new home. Once they entered this promised land, God told them to hang on to a jar of that bread to remind of them how he had provided for them in the past.

Centuries later, Jesus used bread as a reminder too.

"He took some bread and gave thanks to God for it. Then he broke it in pieces and gave it to the disciples, saying, 'This is my body, which is given for you. Do this in remembrance of me'" (Luke 22:19 NLT).

Bread reminds us of good things.

I think it's interesting that Jesus once referred to himself as the Bread of Life. Wherever Jesus went, he brought the aroma of heaven with him. He healed the sick, fed the hungry, cast out evil and raised the dead. He welcomed outcasts and forgave the guilty. He showed us what real love and acceptance looks like.

Jesus smelled like home.

I'm looking forward to being home with him someday and experiencing in full that little taste of heaven I got in my great-grandmother's house on Thanksgiving morning. I don't know if heaven has a door, but if it does, the moment it opens, I know exactly what it will smell like. I've smelled it before. On that day, I will step inside, pull up a chair and take a deep breath, home at last.

Journal Prompts

What are your favorite aromas of Thanksgiving? What pictures or feelings do they stir up in your memory?

How would you describe the perfect home?

What are you looking forward to most about heaven?

God, thank you for the promise of heaven.
I cannot wait to be home with you. Please help me
to be like Jesus and bring the aroma of heaven
everywhere I go today.

Amen

25

TURKEY TALK

If you need wisdom, ask our generous God,
and he will give it to you.

– JAMES 1:5 (NLT)

Several years ago my wife selfishly decided to have a baby close to Thanksgiving, which meant we couldn't travel. This also meant we would host the holiday at our house that year, and someone would have to step up and take responsibility for the turkey. In a further demonstration of my wife's selfishness, that someone ended up being me.

No pressure there, right? I mean it's the turkey, the grand poobah, the big kahuna, the star attraction of the Thanksgiving feast. I was not ready for that kind of responsibility. Let's face it, if you mess up the turkey, not only have you completely tanked the holiday meal but you will become the standard by which all future Thanksgivings in your family will be judged.

"Does this turkey seem a little dry?"

"Not compared to the fiasco of '05! That was drier than the Mojave desert."

"Hey, wasn't that the year we all got our stomach pumped?"

You can see the enormous strain I was under. Sure, my wife was nine months pregnant and ready to pop at any minute, but I had real problems on my hands.

The pressure might have been too much for me, but I had an ace in the hole. The turkey hotline. I figured if worse came to worse I could call up the Butterball people and get them to talk me down off the fridge. I imagined it would be kind of like IT support with poultry.

Sir, you're going to have to reboot the giblets. Just hold down the drumstick for 30 seconds and they should come back online.

Fortunately, it didn't come to that. By what I can only consider a Thanksgiving miracle the turkey turned out so beautiful it would have made Norman Rockwell proud. It turned out that I didn't need my hotline friends after all.

However, the next time I got put in charge of the bird I wasn't taking any chances. I decided to call up the Butterball hotline just to see if they had any helpful tips that would keep me from making a fool of myself.

A few minutes into that phone call I realized I was in the presence of a master.

I talked to a lady we'll call Judy. Judy was like a Navy SEAL with a basting brush. Not only was she incredibly knowledgeable, but she also communicated with an empowering you-can-do-it tone of encouragement. By the time I hung up, she'd convinced me she could solve any problem.

It made me wish they would keep the turkey hotline going all year around and open it up as a call center for personal advice. After all, the holidays aren't the only times we have to deal with turkeys in our lives. Difficult people show up in every season of the year. Wouldn't it be nice to be able to call Judy and ask her how to handle them?

And, of course, if we're honest, sometimes the biggest turkey in the room is us. I know there are days I'd love to call up Judy and ask her how to keep my mouth under control or how to be less selfish or how to be a better husband or dad, but when it comes to that kind of turkey advice, there's only place to go: right into the arms of God.

God is the source of all true wisdom, and he always knows just what to do. He loves us so much that he is constantly available to lead us, correct us and encourage us through even the most challenging moments of life.

So this Thanksgiving, if you're facing a cooking crisis like I was, call Butterball. For your other turkey emergencies, call on God. He's only a prayer away from helping you to have a holiday for which you can truly give thanks.

Journal Prompts

Who is your go-to person when you need advice? Do you think their perspective lines up with God's?

Is prayer your first response in a crisis or more of an afterthought? When you pray, do you do all the talking or take time to listen too?

Are there any turkeys you're dealing with right now that you're not sure how to handle? Is there any of your own turkey behavior you're trying to change?

God, you are the source of all wisdom.
Show me how to access that wisdom to live your way.
Help me to develop the habit of praying in every
situation.

Amen

26

THE BIRTHDAY THAT ATE THANKSGIVING

He fell to the ground at Jesus' feet, thanking him for what he had done.

– LUKE 17:16 (NLT)

Holiday birthdays can be confusing. My oldest daughter's birthday is near Thanksgiving, and several years ago, it fell right on Thanksgiving Day. Because we didn't want her to feel ripped off, we had her birthday party in the morning and ate Thanksgiving dinner with family in the afternoon.

It seemed like a good compromise. While she was sleeping, we decorated the house with princess banners and balloons. Then, we sneaked all of her presents out so we could start celebrating right after breakfast.

She loved it. We had birthday cake for brunch and spent the morning opening gifts and playing.

By the time the extended family arrived, however, we had shifted into full Thanksgiving mode. We served up the turkey and all the trimmings just as the Macy's parade was wrapping up. We'd planned the whole day to perfection. Or so I thought.

That night when I went to tuck my daughter into bed, I asked her, "Honey, did you have a fun Thanksgiving?"

She paused, looked at me like I was crazy and said, "It was Thanksgiving?"

Okay, so maybe we didn't do such a great job of blending birthday and holiday celebrations. My daughter thought the elaborate feast and a house overflowing with family were just for her. The good people of New York City even threw her a big parade.

But if we're honest, she's not the only one this ever happened to. By the time we cook, eat, clean, watch football and cram in whatever other holiday traditions our family has, it can be easy to forget the fact that Thanksgiving is a national day set aside to give thanks for the blessings we all enjoy.

In some seasons it's easier to give thanks than others. Some years our circumstances make it difficult to see the positive in our lives. For most of us, though, we don't neglect Thanksgiving out of bitterness. We neglect it out of busyness. These days we can even get a jump on our holiday shopping before the turkey has grown cold.

I guess on my daughter's birthday I needed to stop and remind her that Thanksgiving is a big deal, not just the holiday, but the habit of expressing gratitude to a God who loves and cares for his kids. On most Thanksgivings I need someone to provide the same reminder for me.

It may sound corny to go around the table expressing what you're thankful for this year. It may feel even more awkward to offer a prayer of thanks to God, but give it a shot and watch the power of thankfulness in action.

True gratitude energizes our spirits by reminding us that Thanksgiving Day, like any other day, isn't about us. We are simply the recipients of blessings and not the source.

Journal Prompts

Do you have any family or friends who tend to make the holidays all about them? Have you ever struggled with this yourself?

What distractions keep you from focusing on gratitude at Thanksgiving?

Are there any new traditions you can build into your family's celebration that will help you stop and give thanks?

God, every day is about you.
Thank you for all of the ways you have blessed my life.
Help me to focus today on your love and goodness.

Amen

27

THANKSGIVING 365

Be thankful in all circumstances, for this is God's will for you who belong to Christ Jesus.

– 1 THESSALONIANS 5:18 (NLT)

When my wife and I first got married, I had this wild, romantic notion to keep a secret thankfulness journal for her. Here's how it was supposed to work. Every day for a year I planned to write down one thing I loved about her. Then I would surprise her the next Christmas with a year's worth of appreciation. I imagined when she opened it, she would swoon, kiss me and then cook me a really nice dinner.

Women love that kind of stuff, right?

So I went out one blustery January day, bought a pink, girly journal and began what I thought would be an easy way to score major points in my marriage.

The first week was awesome. On day eight, however, I had a slight problem. I ran out of material. Now, don't get me wrong. It's not like my wife isn't great, but after about seven days, I thought I had written it all down. I am a guy, after all. We're not exactly wired for sensitivity and emotional intelligence.

My journal went something like this:

Day 1 - You're pretty.

Day 2 – You're nice.

Day 3 – You're pretty nice.

Days four through seven were more of the same. How in the world was I going to fill the other 51 weeks? Surely I could come up with something new to say. I am a writer after all. I have an English degree for crying out loud. Words are supposed to be my thing.
Nope. Nothing.
Maybe I could just give it to her as is. Here you go, honey. Here's one week of wonderful things about you and plenty of blank pages for you to write about how much you love yourself.
Hmm, somehow that didn't seem like the best idea either. I had backed myself into a corner and couldn't see any way out. On day eight I was ready to toss the thankfulness journal into the trash.
But then I had an eureka moment that made Archimedes' bathtub discovery look like child's play. I realized that I was doing this thing all backwards. When I sat down to write in the journal, I was reflecting on the previous day, but nothing stood out because I hadn't been looking for it.
What would happen, I wondered, if I went into each day searching for something I liked about my wife? What would happen if I sought out a quality to admire in her like a miner prospecting for gold? The funny thing was that as I started to pay attention, I began to see things I had totally missed before.
It was like one of those funky 3D pictures that you have to stare at for few minutes before the image appears. Not only did I discover something new to be thankful for in my wife each day, but frequently I found multiple things. Soon, my journal began to overflow.
I was learning to focus what I call my gratitude vision.
The more I discovered, the more I appreciated her, and the more I appreciated, the easier it was for me to see the good stuff. Even on the days we fought, I still came back to that journal, and it forced me to record the things I didn't want to think about when I was pouting. It reminded me that I'd married the best girl in the

world. God used it to correct my attitude over and over again.

At the end of the year, I gave her the journal. And yes, she loved it, but I knew I'd really given myself the best gift of all, the ability to see in advance the things for which I would later be thankful.

What would a year look like if we all kept a thankfulness journal for our lives? What if we went into each day looking for the things for which we would later be thankful? What if we went prospecting for the good gifts of God each and every day? Would it change our attitudes? Would even our worst days glisten with diamonds in the rough?

I wonder if, just as my journal helped me fall more in love with my wife, each of us would fall more in love with life itself and the God who generously gives it.

Journal Prompts

On a scale from 1 to 10, how sharp is your "gratitude vision" right now? Is it easy for you to think of things you're thankful for or do you struggle to come up with much?

What could you do to sharpen that gratitude vision? Keep a daily journal? Set a reminder on your phone? Spend more time with grateful people?

Who is one person you are thankful for today? Why? How can you let them know it?

God, thank you for being so good to me.
Please give me a grateful heart and help me
to pay attention and appreciate the blessings
I experience every day.

Amen

28

MORE THAN WE BARGAINED FOR

Because Jesus was raised from the dead, we've been given
a brand-new life and have everything to live for,
including a future in heaven—and the future starts now!

– 1 PETER 1:3-4 (MSG)

My wife and I went to the mall on Black Friday and got more than we bargained for. She was thirty-eight weeks pregnant so we weren't camping out for flat screen TVs. I just needed to get her out of the house for a few hours.

Personally I had hoped she would go into labor on Thanksgiving Day. How dramatic would that have been? I pictured myself sweeping all of the food off the table and getting ready for an emergency delivery right then and there. We already had family in town, and I had water boiling on the stove while we were cooking the holiday meal. What more did we need?

Unfortunately, my daughter wasn't showing any signs of budging. She wasn't due for another two weeks, and it looked like she was going to hold on until the very last minute. She's still like that when you have to get her up for school.

Once our family had gone home, and Thanksgiving was over, that left us with a fairly boring Black Friday. It wasn't like we even needed to go shopping. My wife had already knocked that out weeks ago and had our presents wrapped and tucked away in the closet.

Still, I thought I'd keep my eye out for a few last minute deals. You never know when you'll find a bargain you just can't pass up. So we went out for lunch and hit the mall. Little did I suspect how dangerous that would be. We hiked from one end of the building to the other and didn't find any bargains, but in the process apparently set the wheels of nature in motion.

About one in the morning my wife woke up with contractions. By ten a.m. my first daughter was born. I'd gone to the mall looking for a bargain, but I ended up coming home with a whole lot more, my own little doorbuster special.

It reminds me of what I experienced when I first began to follow God. Honestly, I went to God looking for a bargain. I was desperate. I was at a low point in my life, and I knew I needed forgiveness and a fresh start. Jesus offered me that for free. He'd already picked up the tab. That was one deal I couldn't pass up.

But it didn't end there. I may have approached God just looking for a bargain, but I walked away with so much more. Little did I suspect the new birth that would follow.

It wasn't just that God wiped away the bad stuff. He adopted me into his family and began to transform me from the inside out. Because God was my Dad in heaven I now had access to all the power and resources at his disposal. My newfound faith wasn't just about a transaction of forgiveness but the beginning of a brand new life.

My wife and I never go shopping on Black Friday anymore. I'm too scared we'll come home with another baby, but every time I drive by the mall during the holiday season, I think about the wonderful surprise of new life in our home that Thanksgiving weekend. And every now and then, it reminds me of the greater surprise of new life in Christ.

Journal Prompts

Has there ever been a time when you've received the free gift of forgiveness from Jesus? If not, what's holding you back?

If you have placed your trust in Jesus, are you experiencing any signs of new life in your heart?

Spend time today thanking God for the bargain of forgiveness he offers you through the cross and ask him to help you grow in new life each and every day.

God, thank you for sending Jesus to die on the cross
for me. I receive that gift of forgiveness today,
but help me not to stop there. Help to walk
in my new life as a part of your family.

Amen

BONUS DEVOTION

29

UNSHAKEABLE CHRISTMAS

God is our refuge and strength,
always ready to help in times of trouble.

– PSALM 46:1 (NLT)

When my wife and I first got married, we used to get our Christmas trees at a fancy tree farm outside of Indianapolis. This place had it all. Not only was it packed with acres of evergreens, but they also had a toy store, a train shop, and even sold hot chocolate to keep you warm.

This was total culture shock for me. I grew up in the country where we usually just cut down the first tree we saw in our backyard for Christmas. Sometimes we would get ambitious and go the local tree farm, which was someone else's back yard. No hot chocolate anywhere in sight.

Of all the innovations of our Indianapolis tree farm, however, none impressed me more than the Christmas tree shaker. Once you bought your tree, they would stick the trunk in this machine to shake out all of the dead needles. This was no gentle process. When the guy working the shaker flipped the switch, it thrashed the tree like a hurricane.

Sometimes I wondered if there would be any needles left when he was done. Would I still have to pay for a bare trunk? Yet, somehow those tiny needles held onto their branches and lasted the better part of the holiday season as long as we kept the tree watered.

Have you ever had one of those Christmases where you feel like you've been through the shaker? I know I have. The hard seasons of life have a way of just shaking the living daylights out of us. Whether it's relationship struggles, work issues, health problems or some other challenge, it seems like by the time we get to the holidays, we may not know which end is up.

I guess that's when we need take a cue from those tenacious trees. When life throws you into the shaker, hold on tight to the branch.

Where can you find a sturdy branch like this? The Old Testament prophets said we need to look no further than the manger. Jeremiah once spoke of a future King called the righteous Branch, a King who would care for his people and lead them with wisdom (Jeremiah 23:5). Isaiah said he would be born of a virgin (Isaiah 7:14) and Micah predicted he would come from the town of Bethlehem (Micah 5:2).

Hundreds of years later this King was born, and millions of people facing some of the hardest circumstances in life are still clinging to him today. Even though you may be in the shaker this Christmas, remember the promise of the Bible that says in Jesus, "all things hold together." (Colossians 1:17 NIV) Even you.

So whether you end up at a fancy tree farm this year or just put up an artificial tree like we do these days, take a moment and remember the sturdy Branch who is strong enough to support you no matter what you're going through today.

Journal Prompts

Have you ever felt like you've been through the Christmas tree shaker? What are the hardest things you've had to deal with during the holidays?

What does it look like for you to cling to Jesus? When have you had to depend on him the most?

Do you know anyone who's facing tough circumstances right now? How can you encourage them in their faith?

God, you are unshakable. Thank you for always being the one solid thing in my life. Help me to cling to you and depend on you no matter what comes my way.

Amen

NOTES

1 Orr, James, M.A., D.D. General Editor, "Entry for 'APPLE, OF THE EYE,'" *International Standard Bible Encyclopedia*, 1915.

2 Rupp, Rebecca, "The Gooey Story of S'mores," *NationalGeographic.com*, August 14, 2015, http://theplate.nationalgeographic.com/2015/08/14/the-gooey-story-of-smores/.

3 "Why Leaves Change Color," *The Northeastern Area USDA Forest Service*, accessed September 15, 2017, https://www.na.fs.fed.us/fhp/pubs/leaves/leaves.shtm.

4 "The Science of Color In Autumn Leaves," *The United States National Arboretum*, accessed September 15, 2017, http://www.usna.usda.gov/PhotoGallery/FallFoliage/ScienceFallColor.html.

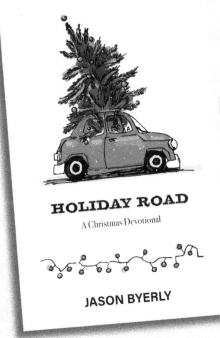